Chicken Alfredo Pasta
A Collection of Delectable and Creamy Pasta Recipes

While every precaution has been taken in the preparation of this book, the publisher assumes no responsibility for errors or omissions, or for damages resulting from the use of the information contained herein.

CHICKEN ALFREDO PASTA

First edition. December 8, 2023.

ISBN: 979-8223980452

Written by john ahmad.

Table of Contents

John Ahmad

Chapter 1: Introduction to Chicken Alfredo Pasta

Section 1: The Rich History of Chicken Alfredo Pasta

Chicken Alfredo Pasta, a dish known for its velvety creamy sauce and tender chunks of chicken, has a fascinating history that spans continents. Its origins can be traced back to Rome, Italy, where it was created by a talented Italian chef named Alfredo di Lelio in the early 20th century. Alfredo originally prepared the dish for his pregnant wife, who was experiencing a loss of appetite. He wanted to create something simple, yet rich and satisfying.

The traditional recipe, known as "Fettuccine Alfredo," consisted of just three main ingredients: fettuccine pasta, butter, and Parmesan cheese. Alfredo's approach was to create a luxurious pasta dish by combining butter and Parmesan to make a silky, creamy sauce, tossing it with freshly cooked fettuccine, and serving it hot. This dish became an instant hit at Alfredo's restaurant in Rome, and it soon garnered attention from international visitors, including several Hollywood celebrities.

Section 2: The Ingredients that Matter

To create the authentic and delicious Chicken Alfredo Pasta, it is crucial to use the right ingredients. Here's what you'll need:

Chicken: Choose boneless, skinless chicken breasts or thighs for a tender and juicy result. You can also use pre-cooked rotisserie chicken for added convenience.

Fettuccine Pasta: Fettuccine, a flat and wide egg-based pasta, is the classic choice for this dish. However, you can experiment with other pasta shapes if you prefer.

Butter: High-quality unsalted butter forms the base of the rich Alfredo sauce, so it's essential to use a good brand.

Heavy Cream: To achieve that luxurious creaminess, opt for heavy cream or whipping cream with a high fat content.

Parmesan Cheese: Use freshly grated Parmesan cheese for the best flavor and texture. Avoid pre-shredded cheese, as it may contain additives that affect the sauce's consistency.

Garlic: Fresh garlic adds a delightful aroma and flavor to the sauce.

Salt and Pepper: Basic seasonings that enhance the overall taste of the dish.

Section 3: Cooking Techniques for Perfect Pasta

To prepare the pasta component of Chicken Alfredo to perfection, follow these steps:

Boil the Water: Fill a large pot with plenty of water and bring it to a rolling boil. Add a generous amount of salt to the water to enhance the pasta's flavor.

Add the Pasta: Gently place the fettuccine into the boiling water and stir to prevent sticking. Cook the pasta until it reaches the desired level of doneness, usually around 8 to 10 minutes for al dente.

Test for Doneness: To check if the pasta is done, taste a small piece. It should be tender but still have a slight firmness in the center.

Drain the Pasta: Once the pasta is cooked, carefully drain it in a colander, reserving a small amount of pasta water to adjust the sauce's consistency later.

Toss with Sauce: Add the drained pasta to the prepared Alfredo sauce and gently toss until the pasta is evenly coated.

Section 4: Preparing the Creamy Alfredo Sauce

Creating the perfect Alfredo sauce is an art that requires attention to detail. Follow these steps for a smooth and velvety sauce:

Melt the Butter: In a large skillet or saucepan over medium heat, melt the butter until it foams slightly.

Saute the Garlic: Add minced garlic to the melted butter and sauté it for about a minute until it becomes fragrant.

Pour in the Cream: Pour the heavy cream into the skillet, stirring constantly to incorporate the butter and garlic flavors.

Simmer and Thicken: Allow the cream to simmer gently for a few minutes until it thickens slightly. Be careful not to let it come to a full boil to avoid curdling.

Add the Parmesan: Gradually add the grated Parmesan cheese to the sauce, stirring continuously until it melts and blends into a creamy consistency.

Season the Sauce: Taste the sauce and season it with salt and freshly ground black pepper according to your preference.

Section 5: Cooking Juicy and Flavorful Chicken

The chicken component of Chicken Alfredo adds protein and flavor to the dish. Follow these steps to cook tender and flavorful chicken:

Season the Chicken: Rub the chicken pieces with salt, pepper, and any additional herbs or seasonings you prefer.

Cook the Chicken: Depending on your chosen method, you can grill, bake, or sauté the chicken until it reaches an internal temperature of 165°F (74°C) for safe consumption.

Slice or Cube the Chicken: Once the chicken is cooked, slice it into thin strips or cube it into bite-sized pieces.

Section 6: Bringing It All Together

Now that you have prepared the pasta, the sauce, and the chicken, it's time to bring everything together into a delicious and comforting plate of Chicken Alfredo Pasta.

Combine the Pasta and Sauce: Add the cooked fettuccine pasta to the skillet with the prepared Alfredo sauce. Toss the pasta gently in the sauce until it is evenly coated.

Add the Chicken: Gently fold in the cooked chicken pieces, ensuring they are well distributed throughout the pasta.

Garnish and Serve: Serve the Chicken Alfredo Pasta hot on individual plates or a large platter. Garnish with a sprinkle of fresh Parmesan cheese, chopped parsley, or crushed red pepper flakes for added flavor and visual appeal.

Chicken Alfredo Pasta is best enjoyed fresh and immediately after preparation, as the creamy sauce tends to thicken upon cooling. However, if you have any leftovers, store them in an airtight container in the refrigerator and reheat on the stovetop or microwave, adding a splash of cream or milk to maintain the creamy consistency.

Chapter 2: Classic Chicken Alfredo
Section 1: The Traditional and Authentic Recipe

In this chapter, we dive into the heart of Chicken Alfredo Pasta—the classic and authentic recipe that has delighted taste buds for generations. This time-tested culinary masterpiece features the rich combination of fettuccine pasta, creamy Alfredo sauce, and tender chicken.

Ingredients:

- 12 ounces (340g) fettuccine pasta
- 2 boneless, skinless chicken breasts (about 1 pound/450g)
- 1/2 cup (1 stick/113g) unsalted butter
- 1 cup (240ml) heavy cream
- 1 cup (100g) grated Parmesan cheese
- 2 cloves garlic, minced
- Salt and freshly ground black pepper to taste
- Fresh parsley, chopped (optional, for garnish)

Instructions:

Cook the Pasta:

In a large pot, bring water to a boil and add a generous amount of salt. Add the fettuccine pasta to the boiling water and cook it according to the package instructions until al dente. Drain the pasta and set it aside, reserving a small amount of pasta water.

Prepare the Chicken:

Season the chicken breasts with salt and pepper on both sides.

Heat a skillet over medium heat and add a drizzle of olive oil. Cook the chicken breasts for about 6-8 minutes per side, or until they reach an internal temperature of 165°F (74°C). Remove the chicken from the skillet and let it rest for a few minutes before slicing it into thin strips.

Make the Alfredo Sauce:

In the same skillet used to cook the chicken, melt the unsalted butter over medium heat.

Add the minced garlic to the melted butter and sauté for about a minute until it becomes aromatic.

Combine the Pasta and Sauce:

Lower the heat to medium-low, and pour the heavy cream into the skillet with the butter and garlic. Stir gently to combine, allowing the cream to heat through.

Add the Parmesan Cheese:

Gradually sprinkle the grated Parmesan cheese into the cream sauce, stirring continuously until the cheese melts completely. The sauce should become thick and creamy.

Toss in the Pasta and Chicken:

Add the cooked fettuccine pasta to the Alfredo sauce, tossing gently to coat the pasta evenly with the sauce.

Gently fold in the sliced chicken, ensuring it is well distributed throughout the pasta.

Season and Garnish:

Taste the Chicken Alfredo Pasta and adjust the seasoning with salt and freshly ground black pepper, if needed.

Garnish with chopped fresh parsley for a burst of color and flavor.

Serve and Enjoy:

Serve the Classic Chicken Alfredo Pasta immediately while it's still hot and at its creamiest best.

Section 2: Tips for the Creamiest Sauce

To achieve the creamiest Alfredo sauce possible, here are some valuable tips to keep in mind:

Use Freshly Grated Parmesan: For the best results, always grate the Parmesan cheese from a block or wheel of Parmigiano-Reggiano. Avoid pre-grated Parmesan, as it may contain additives that affect the sauce's texture and flavor.

Low Heat and Constant Stirring: When combining the cream and Parmesan in the skillet, use low to medium-low heat. Avoid high heat to prevent the sauce from breaking or curdling. Stir continuously as you add the cheese to ensure a smooth and velvety texture.

Don't Overcook the Sauce: The Alfredo sauce thickens quickly, so take care not to overcook it. Once the cheese has melted and the sauce is smooth, remove it from the heat promptly to preserve its creamy consistency.

Reserve Pasta Water: Save a small cup of the starchy pasta water before draining the cooked fettuccine. If the sauce becomes too thick, add a splash of pasta water while tossing the pasta to loosen it up.

Fresh Herbs and Seasonings: Feel free to experiment with fresh herbs and seasonings to enhance the flavors of the sauce. A pinch of nutmeg, a dash of cayenne pepper, or a squeeze of lemon juice can elevate the taste to a whole new level.

By following this authentic recipe and incorporating the tips for a creamy sauce, you'll be savoring the comforting taste of Classic Chicken Alfredo—a dish that has stood the test of time and continues to be cherished by pasta enthusiasts worldwide.

Chapter 3: Garlic Butter Chicken Pasta

Section 1: A Flavorful Twist on the Classic Recipe

In this chapter, we'll explore a delightful variation of the classic Chicken Alfredo Pasta—Garlic Butter Chicken Pasta. By infusing the sauce with the rich flavors of garlic and butter, we elevate this dish to new heights of culinary delight. Get ready to experience a mouthwatering symphony of flavors that will have your taste buds dancing with joy.

Ingredients:

- 12 ounces (340g) fettuccine pasta
- 2 boneless, skinless chicken breasts (about 1 pound/450g)
- 1/2 cup (1 stick/113g) unsalted butter, divided
- 4 cloves garlic, minced
- 1 cup (240ml) heavy cream
- 1 cup (100g) grated Parmesan cheese
- Salt and freshly ground black pepper to taste
- Fresh parsley, chopped (optional, for garnish)

Instructions:

Cook the Pasta:

In a large pot, bring water to a boil and add a generous amount of salt. Cook the fettuccine pasta according to the package instructions until al dente. Drain the pasta and set it aside, reserving a small amount of pasta water.

Prepare the Chicken:

Season the chicken breasts with salt and freshly ground black pepper on both sides.

In a large skillet over medium-high heat, melt 2 tablespoons of butter. Add the seasoned chicken breasts and cook for about 6-8 minutes per side, or until they reach an internal temperature of 165°F (74°C). Remove the chicken from the skillet and let it rest for a few minutes before slicing it into thin strips.

Create the Garlic Butter Sauce:

In the same skillet, melt the remaining butter over medium heat.

Add the minced garlic to the melted butter and sauté for about a minute until it becomes fragrant and lightly golden.

Infuse the Sauce with Flavor:

Pour the heavy cream into the skillet with the garlic butter, stirring gently to combine. Let the mixture simmer for a couple of minutes to allow the flavors to meld.

Thicken the Sauce:

Gradually add the grated Parmesan cheese to the sauce, stirring continuously until the cheese is fully melted and the sauce thickens.

Toss in the Pasta and Chicken:

Add the cooked fettuccine pasta to the garlic butter sauce, tossing gently to coat the pasta evenly.

Gently fold in the sliced chicken, ensuring it is well distributed throughout the pasta.

Season and Garnish:

Taste the Garlic Butter Chicken Pasta and season with additional salt and pepper if needed.

Sprinkle chopped fresh parsley over the dish for a burst of color and a hint of freshness.

Serve and Savor:

Serve the Garlic Butter Chicken Pasta immediately while it's still hot and bursting with flavorful goodness.

Section 2: Incorporating Garlic Butter into the Sauce

Garlic butter is the star of this variation, infusing the sauce with a rich and aromatic flavor that complements the creaminess of the Alfredo sauce. To ensure the garlic butter is perfectly incorporated, consider the following tips:

Finely Mince the Garlic: Finely mince the garlic to release its full flavor. You can also use a garlic press for a finer texture, ensuring the garlic disperses evenly throughout the sauce.

Control the Heat: Keep a watchful eye on the skillet's heat when sautéing the garlic. Overcooking it can result in a bitter taste, so aim for a golden color and a fragrant aroma.

Balance the Butter: The garlic butter sauce should strike a perfect balance between the richness of butter and the creaminess of the Alfredo sauce. Adjust the amount of butter to suit your taste preferences.

By combining the classic components of Chicken Alfredo Pasta with the irresistible allure of garlic butter, you'll create a dish that's sure to become a new favorite at your dining table. Enjoy the harmonious blend of flavors and savor the deliciousness of Garlic Butter Chicken Pasta.

Chapter 4: Grilled Chicken Alfredo Pizza
Section 1: Fusing Italian and American Cuisines

In this chapter, we embark on a culinary adventure by combining the best of Italian and American cuisines to create a mouthwatering Grilled Chicken Alfredo Pizza. This delightful fusion dish brings together the classic flavors of Chicken Alfredo Pasta and the beloved comfort of a pizza, resulting in a unique and irresistible culinary masterpiece.

Ingredients:

- 1 pound (450g) pizza dough (store-bought or homemade)
- 1 cup (240ml) Alfredo sauce (homemade or store-bought)
- 1 cup (100g) shredded mozzarella cheese
- 1 cup (100g) grated Parmesan cheese
- 2 boneless, skinless chicken breasts, grilled and thinly sliced
- 1/2 cup (75g) sliced cherry tomatoes
- 1/4 cup (25g) chopped fresh basil leaves
- 1 tablespoon olive oil
- Salt and freshly ground black pepper to taste
- Red pepper flakes (optional, for added heat)

Instructions:
Preheat the Grill:

Preheat your grill to medium-high heat. Brush the grates with a little oil to prevent sticking.

Grill the Chicken:

Season the chicken breasts with olive oil, salt, and pepper.

Grill the chicken for about 6-8 minutes per side or until cooked through and nicely charred. Let the chicken rest for a few minutes before slicing it into thin strips.

Prepare the Pizza Dough:

On a lightly floured surface, roll out the pizza dough to your desired thickness and shape. Transfer the dough to a pizza peel or a lightly floured baking sheet.

Assemble the Pizza:

Spread a generous amount of Alfredo sauce over the pizza dough, leaving a small border around the edges.

Sprinkle the shredded mozzarella and grated Parmesan cheese evenly over the sauce.

Add the Grilled Chicken and Toppings:

Arrange the grilled chicken strips over the cheese.

Scatter the sliced cherry tomatoes and chopped fresh basil leaves on top.

Grill the Pizza:

Carefully slide the pizza onto the preheated grill. Close the lid and cook the pizza for about 8-10 minutes or until the crust is golden and the cheese has melted.

Finish and Serve:

Remove the pizza from the grill using a pizza peel or tongs.

Drizzle a little olive oil over the pizza and sprinkle with red pepper flakes if desired.

Slice the Grilled Chicken Alfredo Pizza and serve it hot.

Section 2: Creating a Mouthwatering Pizza with Alfredo Sauce

The key to achieving a mouthwatering Grilled Chicken Alfredo Pizza lies in the perfect balance of flavors and textures. Here are some tips to create a delectable pizza with Alfredo sauce:

Choose Quality Ingredients: Opt for high-quality pizza dough, preferably homemade or from a trusted local pizzeria. Select fresh and flavorful toppings, such as ripe cherry tomatoes and fragrant basil leaves, to elevate the overall taste of the pizza.

Homemade Alfredo Sauce: Consider making your Alfredo sauce from scratch for the best results. This allows you to customize the sauce to your liking, adjusting the seasonings and cheese levels for a perfect balance of creaminess and flavor.

Precook the Chicken: Ensure the grilled chicken is fully cooked before adding it to the pizza. Precooking the chicken on the grill imparts a smoky flavor that complements the pizza's overall profile.

Don't Overload the Pizza: While it may be tempting to add a plethora of toppings, remember that less is often more when it comes to pizza. Avoid overloading the pizza with ingredients, as this can weigh down the crust and hinder the cooking process.

Achieve the Perfect Grill Marks: For those sought-after grill marks on the pizza crust, preheat the grill properly and brush the dough with a little olive oil before placing it on the grates.

By merging the delightful creaminess of Alfredo sauce with the familiar comfort of pizza, you'll create a Grilled Chicken Alfredo Pizza that surprises and delights the taste buds. This fusion of Italian and American cuisines is sure to become a favorite for family gatherings and casual dinner parties alike. Enjoy the fusion of flavors, and let your creativity shine when experimenting with toppings to make it uniquely your own.

Chapter 5: Cajun Chicken Alfredo
Section 1: Adding a Spicy Kick to the Dish

In this chapter, we'll explore a fiery twist on the classic Chicken Alfredo Pasta—Cajun Chicken Alfredo. By infusing the dish with the bold and vibrant flavors of Cajun seasoning, we'll take this creamy pasta to a whole new level of excitement. Get ready to tantalize your taste buds with the perfect balance of heat and creaminess in every bite.

Ingredients:

- 12 ounces (340g) fettuccine pasta
- 2 boneless, skinless chicken breasts (about 1 pound/450g)
- 2 tablespoons Cajun seasoning (store-bought or homemade)
- 2 tablespoons olive oil
- 1/2 cup (1 stick/113g) unsalted butter
- 1 cup (240ml) heavy cream
- 1 cup (100g) grated Parmesan cheese
- 2 cloves garlic, minced
- Salt and freshly ground black pepper to taste
- Fresh parsley, chopped (optional, for garnish)

Instructions:

Cook the Pasta:

In a large pot, bring water to a boil and add a generous amount of salt. Cook the fettuccine pasta according to the package instructions until al dente. Drain the pasta and set it aside, reserving a small amount of pasta water.

Prepare the Cajun Chicken:

Season the chicken breasts with Cajun seasoning, making sure to coat them evenly on both sides.

In a skillet over medium-high heat, add olive oil and cook the seasoned chicken for about 6-8 minutes per side, or until it reaches an internal temperature of 165°F (74°C). Remove the chicken from the skillet and let it rest for a few minutes before slicing it into thin strips.

Make the Cajun Alfredo Sauce:

In the same skillet used to cook the chicken, melt the unsalted butter over medium heat.

Add the minced garlic to the melted butter and sauté for about a minute until it becomes fragrant.

Add the Cream and Cajun Seasoning:

Pour the heavy cream into the skillet with the butter and garlic, stirring gently to combine.

Stir in the Cajun seasoning, adjusting the amount to your desired level of spiciness.

Thicken the Sauce:

Gradually add the grated Parmesan cheese to the sauce, stirring continuously until the cheese is fully melted and the sauce thickens.

Toss in the Pasta and Chicken:

Add the cooked fettuccine pasta to the Cajun Alfredo sauce, tossing gently to coat the pasta evenly.

Gently fold in the sliced Cajun chicken, ensuring it is well distributed throughout the pasta.

Season and Garnish:

Taste the Cajun Chicken Alfredo Pasta and season with additional salt and freshly ground black pepper if needed.

Garnish with chopped fresh parsley for a pop of color and a hint of freshness.

Serve and Savor:

Serve the Cajun Chicken Alfredo Pasta immediately while it's still hot, bringing the zesty heat of Cajun seasoning together with the creamy Alfredo sauce.

Section 2: Balancing Flavors with Cajun Seasoning

The key to achieving the perfect Cajun Chicken Alfredo lies in striking the right balance of flavors. Here are some tips to help you achieve that ideal harmony:

Customizing Cajun Seasoning: If using store-bought Cajun seasoning, taste it beforehand to gauge its spiciness and saltiness. Adjust the quantity you add to the sauce based on your personal preference.

Controlling the Spice: For a milder version, use less Cajun seasoning or opt for a mild variety. If you prefer an extra kick, feel free to amp up the spiciness with a hotter Cajun blend or by adding a pinch of cayenne pepper.

Creaminess Counterbalances Heat: The Alfredo sauce's creaminess helps balance the heat from the Cajun seasoning, providing a comforting backdrop to the spice. Adjust the creaminess to your liking by adding a little more heavy cream if desired.

Experiment with Additional Ingredients: For added complexity and depth of flavor, consider incorporating diced bell peppers, onions, or sliced mushrooms to the Cajun Chicken Alfredo. These ingredients complement the Cajun seasoning and create a well-rounded dish.

By marrying the intense flavors of Cajun seasoning with the creamy indulgence of Alfredo sauce, you'll create a Cajun Chicken Alfredo Pasta that's packed with excitement and flavor. Enjoy the fusion of spicy and creamy elements in each delicious forkful, and feel free to adjust the seasoning and heat level to suit your taste preferences.

Chapter 6: Mushroom and Chicken Alfredo

Section 1: A Vegetarian-Friendly Option

In this chapter, we'll explore a vegetarian-friendly twist on the classic Chicken Alfredo Pasta—Mushroom and Chicken Alfredo. By replacing the chicken with hearty mushrooms, we create a delightful meatless version of this beloved dish. The umami-rich mushrooms add depth and texture to the creamy Alfredo sauce, making it a satisfying and flavorful choice for both vegetarians and mushroom lovers alike.

Ingredients:

- 12 ounces (340g) fettuccine pasta
- 8 ounces (225g) cremini mushrooms, sliced
- 1 cup (240ml) vegetable broth
- 1 cup (240ml) heavy cream
- 1/2 cup (1 stick/113g) unsalted butter
- 1 cup (100g) grated Parmesan cheese
- 2 cloves garlic, minced
- 2 tablespoons olive oil
- Salt and freshly ground black pepper to taste
- Fresh parsley, chopped (optional, for garnish)

Instructions:

Cook the Pasta:

In a large pot, bring water to a boil and add a generous amount of salt. Cook the fettuccine pasta according to the package instructions until al dente. Drain the pasta and set it aside, reserving a small amount of pasta water.

Sauté the Mushrooms:

In a large skillet over medium-high heat, add olive oil and sauté the sliced cremini mushrooms until they release their moisture and turn golden brown. Remove half of the mushrooms from the skillet and set them aside for garnish later.

Make the Mushroom Alfredo Sauce:

In the same skillet with the remaining sautéed mushrooms, melt the unsalted butter over medium heat.

Add the minced garlic and cook for about a minute until it becomes fragrant.

Incorporate the Vegetable Broth:

Pour the vegetable broth into the skillet with the butter and garlic, stirring gently to combine. Allow the mixture to simmer for a few minutes to infuse the flavors.

Add the Heavy Cream and Parmesan Cheese:

Stir in the heavy cream, bringing the sauce to a gentle simmer.

Gradually add the grated Parmesan cheese, stirring continuously until the cheese is fully melted and the sauce thickens.

Toss in the Pasta and Mushrooms:

Add the cooked fettuccine pasta to the Mushroom Alfredo sauce, tossing gently to coat the pasta evenly.

Fold in the reserved sautéed mushrooms, ensuring they are well distributed throughout the pasta.

Season and Garnish:

Taste the Mushroom and Chicken Alfredo Pasta and season with salt and freshly ground black pepper to your liking.

Garnish with chopped fresh parsley for a burst of color and a touch of freshness.

Serve and Savor:

Serve the Mushroom and Chicken Alfredo Pasta hot, savoring the delightful combination of creamy Alfredo sauce and earthy mushrooms.

Section 2: Enhancing the Dish with Mushrooms

Mushrooms are a versatile and delightful addition to the traditional Chicken Alfredo Pasta, offering a meaty texture and rich flavor. Here are some tips for enhancing the dish with mushrooms:

Mushroom Selection: Use cremini mushrooms, also known as baby portobello mushrooms, for their meaty texture and deep flavor. Alternatively, you can use white button mushrooms or a combination of different mushroom varieties.

Sautéing Mushrooms: Sautéing the mushrooms in olive oil helps release their moisture, intensifying their flavor and giving them a delicious golden-brown color.

Mushroom Broth: If you prefer an even more intense mushroom flavor, consider using mushroom broth instead of vegetable broth when making the sauce.

Variety of Mushrooms: Experiment with different mushroom types, such as shiitake, oyster, or porcini, to add complexity and variety to the dish.

By embracing the earthy and savory allure of mushrooms, you'll create a Mushroom and Chicken Alfredo Pasta that delights the taste buds with its vegetarian-friendly goodness. Enjoy the velvety creaminess of the Alfredo sauce combined with the satisfying bite of sautéed mushrooms, and savor each delectable forkful of this delightful pasta dish.

Chapter 7: Lemon Pepper Chicken Alfredo

Section 1: Brightening the Flavors with Citrusy Notes

In this chapter, we'll explore a refreshing variation of the classic Chicken Alfredo Pasta—Lemon Pepper Chicken Alfredo. By infusing the dish with the zesty and vibrant flavors of lemon pepper seasoning, we'll add a burst of citrusy goodness to the creamy Alfredo sauce. The combination of the creamy sauce with the bright and tangy lemon pepper creates a delightful symphony of flavors that will awaken your taste buds.

Ingredients:

- 12 ounces (340g) fettuccine pasta
- 2 boneless, skinless chicken breasts (about 1 pound/450g)
- 2 tablespoons lemon pepper seasoning
- 2 tablespoons olive oil
- 1/2 cup (1 stick/113g) unsalted butter
- 1 cup (240ml) heavy cream
- Zest of one lemon
- 1 cup (100g) grated Parmesan cheese
- 2 cloves garlic, minced
- Salt and freshly ground black pepper to taste
- Fresh parsley, chopped (optional, for garnish)
- Lemon slices, for garnish

Instructions:

Cook the Pasta:

In a large pot, bring water to a boil and add a generous amount of salt. Cook the fettuccine pasta according to the package instructions until al dente. Drain the pasta and set it aside, reserving a small amount of pasta water.

Prepare the Lemon Pepper Chicken:

Season the chicken breasts with lemon pepper seasoning, making sure to coat them evenly on both sides.

In a skillet over medium-high heat, add olive oil and cook the seasoned chicken for about 6-8 minutes per side, or until it reaches an internal temperature of 165°F (74°C). Remove the chicken from the skillet and let it rest for a few minutes before slicing it into thin strips.

Create the Lemon Pepper Alfredo Sauce:

In the same skillet used to cook the chicken, melt the unsalted butter over medium heat.

Add the minced garlic to the melted butter and sauté for about a minute until it becomes fragrant.

Infuse the Sauce with Lemon:

Stir in the heavy cream and lemon zest, bringing the sauce to a gentle simmer. The lemon zest will infuse the sauce with a fresh citrus aroma.

Add the Parmesan Cheese:

Gradually add the grated Parmesan cheese to the sauce, stirring continuously until the cheese is fully melted and the sauce thickens.

Toss in the Pasta and Chicken:

Add the cooked fettuccine pasta to the Lemon Pepper Alfredo sauce, tossing gently to coat the pasta evenly.

Fold in the sliced lemon pepper chicken, ensuring it is well distributed throughout the pasta.

Season and Garnish:

Taste the Lemon Pepper Chicken Alfredo Pasta and season with salt and freshly ground black pepper to your liking.

Garnish with chopped fresh parsley and lemon slices for a vibrant and refreshing presentation.

Serve and Savor:

Serve the Lemon Pepper Chicken Alfredo Pasta hot, savoring the harmonious blend of creamy Alfredo sauce with the zesty notes of lemon pepper seasoning.

Section 2: Using Lemon Pepper Seasoning Effectively

Lemon pepper seasoning is a versatile spice blend that combines the brightness of lemon zest with the subtle heat of black pepper. Here are some tips for using lemon pepper seasoning effectively:

Seasoning the Chicken: Lemon pepper seasoning is perfect for seasoning the chicken breasts, infusing them with tangy and peppery flavors during cooking. Ensure even coating on both sides for maximum impact.

Zest of Fresh Lemon: For the Lemon Pepper Alfredo sauce, use freshly grated lemon zest to bring a bright and natural citrus flavor to the dish.

Adjusting the Lemon Pepper: Taste the sauce after adding the lemon pepper seasoning to gauge the level of citrusy tang and spiciness. If you prefer a stronger lemon flavor, you can add a little more lemon zest or lemon juice.

Complementing Ingredients: Consider adding a sprinkle of lemon pepper seasoning to the sauce or the pasta itself for an extra burst of flavor.

By incorporating the lively essence of lemon pepper seasoning, you'll create a Lemon Pepper Chicken Alfredo Pasta that captivates your taste buds with its tantalizing blend of creaminess and citrusy brightness. Enjoy the refreshing notes of lemon pepper, and let it bring a refreshing twist to the classic Chicken Alfredo.

Chapter 8: One-Pot Chicken Alfredo
Section 1: Simplifying the Cooking Process

In this chapter, we'll explore a time-saving and convenient version of Chicken Alfredo Pasta—One-Pot Chicken Alfredo. By preparing the entire dish in a single pot, we simplify the cooking process, making it a breeze to create this comforting and creamy pasta meal. This method not only saves time but also minimizes cleanup, making it perfect for busy weeknights or whenever you're looking for an easy, delicious meal.

Ingredients:

- 12 ounces (340g) fettuccine pasta
- 2 boneless, skinless chicken breasts (about 1 pound/450g), cut into bite-sized pieces
- 4 cups (960ml) chicken broth
- 1 cup (240ml) heavy cream
- 1/2 cup (1 stick/113g) unsalted butter
- 1 cup (100g) grated Parmesan cheese
- 2 cloves garlic, minced
- Salt and freshly ground black pepper to taste
- Fresh parsley, chopped (optional, for garnish)

Instructions:

Combine Ingredients in the Pot:

In a large pot or Dutch oven, add the fettuccine pasta, chicken pieces, chicken broth, heavy cream, and unsalted butter.

Cook the One-Pot Chicken Alfredo:

Place the pot on the stove over medium-high heat. Stir the ingredients to combine, making sure the pasta is fully submerged in the liquid.

Simmer and Stir:

Bring the mixture to a boil, then reduce the heat to a simmer. Stir occasionally to prevent the pasta from sticking together.

Check for Doneness:

Cook the One-Pot Chicken Alfredo until the pasta is cooked to your desired level of doneness and the chicken is cooked through.

Add Parmesan Cheese and Seasoning:

Once the pasta and chicken are cooked, stir in the grated Parmesan cheese, minced garlic, salt, and freshly ground black pepper.

Final Touches:

Continue stirring until the cheese is fully melted, and the sauce becomes creamy and smooth.

Garnish and Serve:

Remove the pot from the heat and let it rest for a minute. The sauce will thicken slightly upon standing.

Garnish with chopped fresh parsley for a burst of color and freshness.

Serve and Enjoy:

Serve the One-Pot Chicken Alfredo immediately while it's hot, savoring the rich creaminess and the convenience of a single-pot meal.

Section 2: Minimizing Cleanup with a Single Pot

The beauty of One-Pot Chicken Alfredo lies not only in its simplicity but also in the minimal cleanup required. Here are some tips to make the process even smoother:

Non-Stick Pot: Use a non-stick pot or a well-seasoned Dutch oven to prevent the pasta from sticking to the bottom.

Stirring Regularly: Stir the pasta occasionally to ensure even cooking and prevent it from clumping together.

Customize Ingredients: Feel free to add your favorite vegetables, such as broccoli, peas, or spinach, to make it a complete one-pot meal.

Adjust Liquid Levels: Depending on the type of pasta you use and your desired consistency, you may need to adjust the amount of chicken broth and heavy cream.

By embracing the simplicity of the one-pot cooking method, you'll create a delightful and creamy Chicken Alfredo Pasta with minimal effort and cleanup. This approach is perfect for busy days when you want to enjoy a comforting and delicious meal without the hassle of multiple pots and pans. Sit back, relax, and savor the convenience of One-Pot Chicken Alfredo!

Chapter 9: Broccoli and Chicken Alfredo

Section 1: Incorporating Greens for a Nutritious Twist

In this chapter, we'll explore a wholesome variation of Chicken Alfredo Pasta—Broccoli and Chicken Alfredo. By adding nutritious broccoli to the dish, we elevate its health benefits and create a satisfying meal that's both creamy and packed with greens. This flavorful twist not only enhances the taste but also adds a vibrant touch of color to the dish.

Ingredients:

- 12 ounces (340g) fettuccine pasta
- 2 boneless, skinless chicken breasts (about 1 pound/450g), cut into bite-sized pieces
- 2 cups broccoli florets
- 1 cup (240ml) chicken broth
- 1 cup (240ml) heavy cream
- 1/2 cup (1 stick/113g) unsalted butter
- 1 cup (100g) grated Parmesan cheese
- 2 cloves garlic, minced
- Salt and freshly ground black pepper to taste
- Red pepper flakes (optional, for added heat)
- Fresh parsley, chopped (optional, for garnish)

Instructions:

Cook the Pasta and Broccoli:

In a large pot, bring water to a boil and add a generous amount of salt. Add the fettuccine pasta and cook according to the package instructions until al dente.

During the last 3 minutes of cooking the pasta, add the broccoli florets to the boiling water and cook until they are tender-crisp. Drain the pasta and broccoli together and set them aside, reserving a small amount of pasta water.

Prepare the Chicken:

Season the chicken pieces with salt and freshly ground black pepper.

In a skillet over medium-high heat, add a drizzle of olive oil. Cook the seasoned chicken for about 6-8 minutes per side, or until it reaches an internal temperature of 165°F (74°C). Remove the chicken from the skillet and set it aside.

Make the Broccoli and Chicken Alfredo Sauce:

In the same skillet used to cook the chicken, melt the unsalted butter over medium heat.

Add the minced garlic and sauté for about a minute until it becomes fragrant.

Add the Chicken Broth and Heavy Cream:

Pour the chicken broth into the skillet with the butter and garlic, stirring gently to combine.

Stir in the heavy cream and let the mixture simmer for a few minutes to thicken slightly.

Incorporate the Parmesan Cheese and Seasoning:

Gradually add the grated Parmesan cheese to the sauce, stirring continuously until the cheese is fully melted and the sauce becomes creamy and smooth.

Season the sauce with salt and freshly ground black pepper to your liking. For those who enjoy some heat, sprinkle red pepper flakes into the sauce.

Toss in the Pasta, Broccoli, and Chicken:
Add the cooked fettuccine pasta, broccoli florets, and chicken pieces to the Alfredo sauce, tossing gently to coat everything evenly.

Garnish and Serve:
Garnish the Broccoli and Chicken Alfredo Pasta with chopped fresh parsley for added color and a touch of freshness.

Serve and Enjoy:
Serve the Broccoli and Chicken Alfredo hot, savoring the nutritious twist of greens combined with the creamy, savory goodness.

Section 2: Cooking Broccoli to Perfection

Cooking broccoli to the right doneness is crucial to preserve its vibrant color, texture, and nutrients. Here's how to cook broccoli to perfection:

Blanching Method: To preserve the bright green color and tender-crisp texture of broccoli, blanch it in boiling salted water for about 2-3 minutes. Plunge the blanched broccoli into ice-cold water to halt the cooking process and retain its color.

Tasting for Doneness: The broccoli should be tender enough to eat, but not mushy. Taste a piece during the last minute of blanching to ensure it's cooked to your desired level of doneness.

Drain and Shock: Immediately drain the broccoli after blanching and place it in a bowl of ice water for a few seconds to stop the cooking and lock in its vibrant green color.

By incorporating nutrient-rich broccoli into the Chicken Alfredo Pasta, you'll create a wholesome and satisfying dish that's as delicious as it is nutritious. Enjoy the delightful combination of creamy Alfredo sauce, tender-crisp broccoli, and flavorful chicken. This Broccoli and Chicken Alfredo will become a go-to recipe for nourishing and comforting meals that please both the taste buds and the body.

Chapter 10: Pesto Chicken Alfredo
Section 1: Marrying Two Classic Italian Sauces

In this chapter, we'll explore a delectable fusion of two beloved Italian sauces—Pesto Chicken Alfredo. By combining the vibrant flavors of pesto with the creamy richness of Alfredo sauce, we create a harmonious marriage that elevates this pasta dish to a new level of culinary delight. Get ready to experience a burst of herbal freshness and velvety creaminess in every mouthful.

Ingredients:

- 12 ounces (340g) fettuccine pasta
- 2 boneless, skinless chicken breasts (about 1 pound/450g), cut into bite-sized pieces
- 1 cup homemade basil pesto (see instructions below)
- 1 cup (240ml) heavy cream
- 1/2 cup (1 stick/113g) unsalted butter
- 1 cup (100g) grated Parmesan cheese
- 2 cloves garlic, minced
- Salt and freshly ground black pepper to taste
- Fresh basil leaves, for garnish

Instructions:

Cook the Pasta and Prepare the Pesto Chicken:

In a large pot, bring water to a boil and add a generous amount of salt. Cook the fettuccine pasta according to the package instructions until al dente.

While the pasta cooks, season the chicken pieces with salt and freshly ground black pepper.

Make the Pesto:

Prepare the homemade basil pesto (see instructions below) while the pasta is cooking.

Cook the Chicken:

In a skillet over medium-high heat, add a drizzle of olive oil. Cook the seasoned chicken for about 6-8 minutes per side, or until it reaches an internal temperature of 165°F (74°C). Remove the chicken from the skillet and set it aside.

Create the Pesto Alfredo Sauce:

In the same skillet used to cook the chicken, melt the unsalted butter over medium heat.

Add the minced garlic and sauté for about a minute until it becomes fragrant.

Add the Heavy Cream and Pesto:

Stir in the heavy cream, bringing the sauce to a gentle simmer.

Spoon the homemade basil pesto into the sauce, blending it well with the cream.

Thicken the Sauce:

Gradually add the grated Parmesan cheese to the sauce, stirring continuously until the cheese is fully melted and the sauce thickens.

Toss in the Pasta and Chicken:

Add the cooked fettuccine pasta to the Pesto Alfredo sauce, tossing gently to coat the pasta evenly.

Fold in the cooked chicken pieces, ensuring they are well distributed throughout the pasta.

Season and Garnish:

Taste the Pesto Chicken Alfredo Pasta and season with salt and freshly ground black pepper to your liking.

Serve and Enjoy:

Serve the Pesto Chicken Alfredo hot, garnishing with fresh basil leaves for an aromatic and visually appealing presentation.

Section 2: Making Homemade Basil Pesto

Homemade basil pesto adds a burst of freshness and flavor to the Pesto Chicken Alfredo. Here's a simple recipe to prepare this classic sauce:

Ingredients:

- 2 cups fresh basil leaves, packed
- 1/2 cup grated Parmesan cheese
- 1/2 cup pine nuts or walnuts
- 3 garlic cloves
- 1/2 cup extra-virgin olive oil
- Salt and freshly ground black pepper to taste

Instructions:

Blend the Basil and Nuts:

In a food processor, combine the fresh basil leaves, grated Parmesan cheese, pine nuts or walnuts, and garlic cloves.

Drizzle in the Olive Oil:

With the food processor running, gradually drizzle in the extra-virgin olive oil until the mixture becomes a smooth and creamy paste.

Season to Taste:

Add salt and freshly ground black pepper to taste, adjusting the seasoning to your preference.

Store the Pesto:

Transfer the homemade basil pesto to a jar or airtight container. You can refrigerate it for up to a week or freeze it for longer storage.

By preparing the homemade basil pesto and combining it with the creamy Alfredo sauce, you'll create a Pesto Chicken Alfredo Pasta that delights the senses with its vibrant and complementary flavors. Enjoy the delightful union of these classic Italian sauces and savor the freshness and creaminess in every bite. This Pesto Chicken Alfredo is a true celebration of Italian culinary excellence.

Chapter 11: Spinach and Artichoke Chicken Alfredo

Section 1: Infusing the Dish with Richness and Texture

In this chapter, we'll explore a luxurious variation of Chicken Alfredo Pasta—Spinach and Artichoke Chicken Alfredo. By incorporating a luscious spinach and artichoke filling into the dish, we enhance the creaminess and add a delightful texture to the pasta. Get ready to indulge in the velvety Alfredo sauce combined with the richness of the spinach and the unique flavor of artichokes.

Ingredients:

- 12 ounces (340g) fettuccine pasta
- 2 boneless, skinless chicken breasts (about 1 pound/450g), cut into bite-sized pieces
- 1 cup frozen chopped spinach, thawed and drained
- 1 cup canned artichoke hearts, drained and chopped
- 1 cup (240ml) chicken broth
- 1 cup (240ml) heavy cream
- 1/2 cup (1 stick/113g) unsalted butter
- 1 cup (100g) grated Parmesan cheese
- 2 cloves garlic, minced
- Salt and freshly ground black pepper to taste
- Crushed red pepper flakes (optional, for added heat)
- Fresh parsley, chopped (optional, for garnish)

Instructions:
Cook the Pasta and Prepare the Filling:

In a large pot, bring water to a boil and add a generous amount of salt. Cook the fettuccine pasta according to the package instructions until al dente.

While the pasta cooks, prepare the spinach and artichoke filling.

Sauté the Chicken:

In a skillet over medium-high heat, add a drizzle of olive oil. Cook the seasoned chicken for about 6-8 minutes per side, or until it reaches an internal temperature of 165°F (74°C). Remove the chicken from the skillet and set it aside.

Make the Spinach and Artichoke Filling:

In the same skillet used to cook the chicken, melt the unsalted butter over medium heat.

Add the minced garlic and sauté for about a minute until it becomes fragrant.

Add the Spinach and Artichokes:

Stir in the chopped spinach and artichoke hearts, allowing them to cook for a couple of minutes to meld the flavors.

Simmer with Chicken Broth and Heavy Cream:

Pour the chicken broth into the skillet with the spinach and artichokes, stirring gently to combine.

Stir in the heavy cream and let the mixture simmer for a few minutes to thicken slightly.

Incorporate the Parmesan Cheese and Seasoning:

Gradually add the grated Parmesan cheese to the filling, stirring continuously until the cheese is fully melted, and the sauce becomes creamy.

Toss in the Pasta and Chicken:

Add the cooked fettuccine pasta to the Spinach and Artichoke Alfredo sauce, tossing gently to coat the pasta evenly.

Fold in the cooked chicken pieces, ensuring they are well distributed throughout the pasta and filling.

Season and Garnish:

Taste the Spinach and Artichoke Chicken Alfredo Pasta and season with salt and freshly ground black pepper to your liking.

For those who enjoy some heat, sprinkle crushed red pepper flakes into the pasta.

Garnish and Serve:

Garnish the Spinach and Artichoke Chicken Alfredo with chopped fresh parsley for an added burst of color and freshness.

Serve and Enjoy:

Serve the Spinach and Artichoke Chicken Alfredo hot, savoring the richness and texture of the creamy Alfredo sauce combined with the spinach and artichoke filling.

Section 2: Preparing Spinach and Artichoke Filling

The spinach and artichoke filling adds a layer of richness and texture to the Chicken Alfredo Pasta. Here's how to prepare it:

Ingredients:

- 1 tablespoon olive oil
- 2 cloves garlic, minced
- 1 cup frozen chopped spinach, thawed and drained
- 1 cup canned artichoke hearts, drained and chopped
- Salt and freshly ground black pepper to taste

Instructions:

Sauté Garlic and Artichokes:

In a skillet over medium-high heat, add olive oil and minced garlic. Sauté for about a minute until the garlic becomes fragrant.

Add Spinach and Artichokes:

Stir in the chopped spinach and artichoke hearts, allowing them to cook for a couple of minutes to combine the flavors.

Season with salt and freshly ground black pepper to taste.

By preparing the flavorful spinach and artichoke filling and infusing it into the Alfredo sauce, you'll create a Spinach and Artichoke Chicken Alfredo Pasta that's rich, textured, and incredibly satisfying. Enjoy the delightful combination of creamy Alfredo sauce with the earthy spinach and the distinct taste of artichokes. This indulgent dish is sure to become a favorite for special occasions or whenever you crave a truly luxurious pasta experience.

Chapter 12: Chicken Alfredo Stuffed Shells

Section 1: Getting Creative with Pasta Shapes

In this chapter, we'll explore a fun and creative twist on the classic Chicken Alfredo Pasta—Chicken Alfredo Stuffed Shells. By using jumbo pasta shells as a delightful vehicle for the creamy chicken filling, we create a visually appealing and delicious dish that's sure to impress family and guests alike. Let's dive into the world of stuffed shells and enjoy the fusion of flavors and textures.

Ingredients:

- 20 jumbo pasta shells
- 2 boneless, skinless chicken breasts (about 1 pound/450g), cooked and shredded
- 1 cup ricotta cheese
- 1 cup grated mozzarella cheese
- 1/2 cup grated Parmesan cheese
- 1/4 cup chopped fresh parsley
- 1 egg, lightly beaten
- 2 cups Alfredo sauce (homemade or store-bought)
- Salt and freshly ground black pepper to taste
- Olive oil, for greasing the baking dish
- Fresh basil leaves, for garnish

Instructions:
Cook the Jumbo Pasta Shells:
In a large pot, bring water to a boil and add a generous amount of salt. Cook the jumbo pasta shells according to the package instructions until they are al dente. Drain the shells and set them aside.

Prepare the Chicken Alfredo Filling:

In a large mixing bowl, combine the cooked and shredded chicken with ricotta cheese, grated mozzarella cheese, grated Parmesan cheese, chopped fresh parsley, and the lightly beaten egg. Mix everything well until the filling is thoroughly combined.

Season the filling with salt and freshly ground black pepper to taste.

Stuff the Pasta Shells:

Preheat the oven to 375°F (190°C).

Lightly grease a large baking dish with olive oil to prevent sticking.

Spoon a generous amount of the Chicken Alfredo filling into each jumbo pasta shell, making sure to stuff them without overstuffing.

Assemble the Chicken Alfredo Stuffed Shells:

Arrange the stuffed shells in a single layer in the greased baking dish.

Pour the Alfredo sauce over the stuffed shells, covering them evenly.

Bake the Chicken Alfredo Stuffed Shells:

Cover the baking dish with foil and bake in the preheated oven for about 25-30 minutes, or until the filling is heated through and the cheese is melted and bubbly.

Garnish and Serve:

Remove the foil, and if desired, place the baking dish under the broiler for a couple of minutes to lightly brown the top.

Garnish the Chicken Alfredo Stuffed Shells with fresh basil leaves for a fragrant and visually appealing finish.

Serve and Enjoy:

Serve the Chicken Alfredo Stuffed Shells hot, savoring the delightful combination of tender pasta shells, creamy chicken filling, and the velvety Alfredo sauce.

Section 2: Stuffing Shells with Chicken Alfredo Mixture

Stuffing shells with the chicken Alfredo mixture requires a bit of care and precision. Here are some tips to ensure success:

Handling the Pasta Shells: Cook the jumbo pasta shells until they are slightly undercooked (al dente) to make them more pliable for stuffing. Drain and rinse them in cold water to prevent them from sticking together.

Filling the Shells: Using a small spoon or your fingers, gently stuff the Chicken Alfredo filling into each pasta shell, ensuring they are filled evenly without breaking the shells.

Avoid Overstuffing: Be mindful not to overstuff the shells to prevent them from bursting during baking. The filling will expand slightly as it cooks, so leave some space in the shells.

Neat Arrangement: Place the stuffed shells in a single layer in the baking dish, allowing them to cook evenly and ensuring the sauce covers each shell adequately.

By getting creative with pasta shapes and stuffing shells with the delightful Chicken Alfredo mixture, you'll create a visually appealing and scrumptious dish that delights both the eyes and taste buds. Enjoy the fusion of creamy filling, tender pasta shells, and the luxurious Alfredo sauce. The Chicken Alfredo Stuffed Shells will quickly become a favorite addition to your pasta repertoire.

Chapter 13: Bacon and Ranch Chicken Alfredo

Section 1: Combining Favorite Flavors for a Comfort Food

In this chapter, we'll explore a comforting and flavorful variation of Chicken Alfredo Pasta—Bacon and Ranch Chicken Alfredo. By combining the beloved tastes of ranch seasoning and crispy bacon with the creamy Alfredo sauce, we create a dish that's a true comfort food favorite. Prepare to indulge in the rich and savory goodness of this delicious pasta creation.

Ingredients:

- 12 ounces (340g) fettuccine pasta
- 2 boneless, skinless chicken breasts (about 1 pound/450g), cut into bite-sized pieces
- 6 slices bacon, cooked until crispy and crumbled
- 1 cup (240ml) chicken broth
- 1 cup (240ml) heavy cream
- 1/2 cup (1 stick/113g) unsalted butter
- 1 cup (100g) grated Parmesan cheese
- 2 tablespoons ranch seasoning mix (homemade or store-bought)
- 2 cloves garlic, minced
- Salt and freshly ground black pepper to taste
- Fresh parsley, chopped (optional, for garnish)

Instructions:
Cook the Pasta and Prepare the Chicken:

In a large pot, bring water to a boil and add a generous amount of salt. Cook the fettuccine pasta according to the package instructions until al dente.

While the pasta cooks, season the chicken pieces with salt and freshly ground black pepper.

Cook the Bacon:

In a separate skillet, cook the bacon until crispy. Once cooked, crumble the bacon into small pieces and set it aside.

Sauté the Chicken:

In the same skillet used to cook the bacon, add a drizzle of olive oil if needed. Cook the seasoned chicken for about 6-8 minutes per side, or until it reaches an internal temperature of 165°F (74°C). Remove the chicken from the skillet and set it aside.

Create the Ranch Alfredo Sauce:

In the same skillet used to cook the bacon and chicken, melt the unsalted butter over medium heat.

Add the minced garlic and sauté for about a minute until it becomes fragrant.

Incorporate the Chicken Broth and Heavy Cream:

Stir in the chicken broth, scraping any browned bits from the bottom of the skillet for added flavor.

Stir in the heavy cream and let the mixture simmer for a few minutes to thicken slightly.

Add the Ranch Seasoning:

Sprinkle the ranch seasoning mix into the sauce, adjusting the amount to your preference. Ranch seasoning typically contains herbs and spices like garlic, onion, dill, and parsley, which add a delightful flavor profile to the dish.

Thicken the Sauce:

Gradually add the grated Parmesan cheese to the sauce, stirring continuously until the cheese is fully melted and the sauce becomes creamy.

Toss in the Pasta, Chicken, and Bacon:

Add the cooked fettuccine pasta to the Ranch Alfredo sauce, tossing gently to coat the pasta evenly.

Fold in the cooked chicken pieces and crumbled bacon, ensuring they are well distributed throughout the pasta and sauce.

Season and Garnish:
Taste the Bacon and Ranch Chicken Alfredo Pasta and season with salt and freshly ground black pepper to your liking.

Serve and Enjoy:
Serve the Bacon and Ranch Chicken Alfredo hot, garnishing with chopped fresh parsley for added color and a touch of freshness.

Section 2: Incorporating Ranch Seasoning and Bacon

Ranch seasoning and bacon add a delicious twist to the classic Chicken Alfredo Pasta. Here's how to incorporate them effectively:

Ranch Seasoning: Ranch seasoning is widely available in stores, or you can make your own by combining dried herbs like parsley, dill, chives, garlic powder, onion powder, salt, and pepper. Adjust the amount of ranch seasoning to your taste preference for a mild or bold ranch flavor.

Crispy Bacon: Cook the bacon until it's crispy and then crumble it into small pieces before incorporating it into the Chicken Alfredo Pasta. The crispy bacon adds a delightful crunch and smoky flavor to the dish.

By combining the delightful flavors of ranch seasoning and crispy bacon with the creamy Alfredo sauce, you'll create a Bacon and Ranch Chicken Alfredo Pasta that's a comforting and flavorful feast. Enjoy the indulgent combination of creamy sauce, savory chicken, and the delectable addition of ranch and bacon. This dish will quickly become a go-to comfort food favorite for any occasion.

Chapter 14: Sun-Dried Tomato Chicken Alfredo

Section 1: Intensifying Flavors with Sun-Dried Tomatoes

In this chapter, we'll explore a robust and flavorful variation of Chicken Alfredo Pasta—Sun-Dried Tomato Chicken Alfredo. By incorporating the intense flavors of sun-dried tomatoes, we elevate the dish with a burst of tanginess and a hint of sweetness. Get ready to enjoy the delightful combination of creamy Alfredo sauce, tender chicken, and the rich taste of sun-dried tomatoes.

Ingredients:

- 12 ounces (340g) fettuccine pasta
- 2 boneless, skinless chicken breasts (about 1 pound/450g), cut into bite-sized pieces
- 1 cup sun-dried tomatoes (packed in oil or dry), chopped
- 1 cup (240ml) chicken broth
- 1 cup (240ml) heavy cream
- 1/2 cup (1 stick/113g) unsalted butter
- 1 cup (100g) grated Parmesan cheese
- 2 cloves garlic, minced
- Salt and freshly ground black pepper to taste
- Fresh basil leaves, chopped (optional, for garnish)

Instructions:

Cook the Pasta and Prepare the Chicken:

In a large pot, bring water to a boil and add a generous amount of salt. Cook the fettuccine pasta according to the package instructions until al dente.

While the pasta cooks, season the chicken pieces with salt and freshly ground black pepper.

Sauté the Chicken:

In a skillet over medium-high heat, add a drizzle of olive oil. Cook the seasoned chicken for about 6-8 minutes per side, or until it reaches an internal temperature of 165°F (74°C). Remove the chicken from the skillet and set it aside.

Create the Sun-Dried Tomato Alfredo Sauce:

In the same skillet used to cook the chicken, melt the unsalted butter over medium heat.

Add the minced garlic and sauté for about a minute until it becomes fragrant.

Incorporate the Chicken Broth and Heavy Cream:

Stir in the chicken broth, scraping any browned bits from the bottom of the skillet for added flavor.

Stir in the heavy cream and let the mixture simmer for a few minutes to thicken slightly.

Add the Sun-Dried Tomatoes:

Fold in the chopped sun-dried tomatoes, allowing them to rehydrate and infuse the sauce with their rich flavors.

Thicken the Sauce:

Gradually add the grated Parmesan cheese to the sauce, stirring continuously until the cheese is fully melted and the sauce becomes creamy.

Toss in the Pasta and Chicken:

Add the cooked fettuccine pasta to the Sun-Dried Tomato Alfredo sauce, tossing gently to coat the pasta evenly.

Fold in the cooked chicken pieces, ensuring they are well distributed throughout the pasta and sauce.

Season and Garnish:

Taste the Sun-Dried Tomato Chicken Alfredo Pasta and season with salt and freshly ground black pepper to your liking.

Garnish and Serve:

Garnish the Sun-Dried Tomato Chicken Alfredo with chopped fresh basil leaves for an added burst of color and freshness.

Serve and Enjoy:

Serve the Sun-Dried Tomato Chicken Alfredo hot, savoring the robust flavors of the sun-dried tomatoes combined with the creamy Alfredo sauce.

Section 2: Choosing the Right Type of Sun-Dried Tomatoes

When making Sun-Dried Tomato Chicken Alfredo, you have options when it comes to the type of sun-dried tomatoes:

Sun-Dried Tomatoes in Oil: These sun-dried tomatoes are preserved in oil, which gives them a soft and chewy texture. They have a rich, intense flavor and are ready to use right out of the jar.

Dry Sun-Dried Tomatoes: These are sun-dried tomatoes without any oil, typically sold in sealed bags. To use them, you'll need to rehydrate them before adding them to the dish. Simply soak them in warm water for about 20-30 minutes until they become plump and tender.

Both types of sun-dried tomatoes work well in this dish, so choose the one that best suits your taste and convenience. The sun-dried tomatoes will add a delightful tangy and sweet note to the Chicken Alfredo Pasta, making it a memorable and flavorful experience. Enjoy the delectable combination of creamy sauce, tender chicken, and the richness of sun-dried tomatoes.

Chapter 15: Creamy Garlic Parmesan Chicken Pasta

Section 1: Adding a Parmesan Twist to the Sauce

In this chapter, we'll explore a delightful variation of Chicken Alfredo Pasta—Creamy Garlic Parmesan Chicken Pasta. By incorporating the nutty and savory flavors of Parmesan cheese into the creamy sauce, we create a dish that's rich, satisfying, and bursting with cheesy goodness. Prepare to indulge in the creamy, garlicky goodness of this irresistible pasta creation.

Ingredients:

- 12 ounces (340g) fettuccine pasta
- 2 boneless, skinless chicken breasts (about 1 pound/450g), cut into bite-sized pieces
- 1 cup (240ml) chicken broth
- 1 cup (240ml) heavy cream
- 1/2 cup (1 stick/113g) unsalted butter
- 1 cup (100g) grated Parmesan cheese
- 4 cloves garlic, minced
- Salt and freshly ground black pepper to taste
- Fresh parsley, chopped (optional, for garnish)

Instructions:

Cook the Pasta and Prepare the Chicken:

In a large pot, bring water to a boil and add a generous amount of salt. Cook the fettuccine pasta according to the package instructions until al dente.

While the pasta cooks, season the chicken pieces with salt and freshly ground black pepper.

Sauté the Chicken:

In a skillet over medium-high heat, add a drizzle of olive oil. Cook the seasoned chicken for about 6-8 minutes per side, or until it reaches an internal temperature of 165°F (74°C). Remove the chicken from the skillet and set it aside.

Create the Creamy Garlic Parmesan Sauce:

In the same skillet used to cook the chicken, melt the unsalted butter over medium heat.

Add the minced garlic and sauté for about a minute until it becomes fragrant.

Incorporate the Chicken Broth and Heavy Cream:

Stir in the chicken broth, scraping any browned bits from the bottom of the skillet for added flavor.

Stir in the heavy cream and let the mixture simmer for a few minutes to thicken slightly.

Add the Parmesan Cheese:

Gradually add the grated Parmesan cheese to the sauce, stirring continuously until the cheese is fully melted, and the sauce becomes creamy and smooth.

Toss in the Pasta and Chicken:

Add the cooked fettuccine pasta to the Creamy Garlic Parmesan sauce, tossing gently to coat the pasta evenly.

Fold in the cooked chicken pieces, ensuring they are well distributed throughout the pasta and sauce.

Season and Garnish:

Taste the Creamy Garlic Parmesan Chicken Pasta and season with salt and freshly ground black pepper to your liking.

Garnish and Serve:

Garnish the Creamy Garlic Parmesan Chicken Pasta with chopped fresh parsley for an added burst of color and freshness.

Serve and Enjoy:

Serve the Creamy Garlic Parmesan Chicken Pasta hot, savoring the rich and cheesy flavors combined with the creamy Alfredo sauce.

Section 2: Balancing Garlic and Cheese Flavors

To achieve a well-balanced Creamy Garlic Parmesan Chicken Pasta, it's essential to find the right ratio of garlic and Parmesan cheese flavors. Here are some tips:

Adjusting Garlic: The recipe calls for four cloves of minced garlic, but you can adjust the amount based on your preference. If you enjoy a stronger garlic flavor, you can add more cloves. Conversely, if you prefer a milder garlic taste, you can reduce the amount of garlic.

Enhancing Parmesan Cheese: The grated Parmesan cheese adds a distinct nutty and savory taste to the dish. If you want a more pronounced Parmesan flavor, you can add an extra sprinkle of grated Parmesan on top before serving.

By balancing the garlic and cheese flavors effectively, you'll create a Creamy Garlic Parmesan Chicken Pasta that's a delightful harmony of creamy, cheesy goodness with a garlicky kick. Enjoy the comforting and satisfying experience of this pasta dish, and savor the luxurious combination of the creamy Alfredo sauce, tender chicken, and the rich flavors of garlic and Parmesan cheese.

Chapter 16: Chicken Alfredo Lasagna
Section 1: Layering Pasta and Sauce for a Hearty Dish

In this chapter, we'll explore a hearty and indulgent variation of Chicken Alfredo Pasta—Chicken Alfredo Lasagna. By layering lasagna noodles with the creamy Alfredo sauce and savory chicken, we create a comforting and satisfying dish that's perfect for gatherings or special occasions. Prepare to enjoy the richness of this delicious lasagna creation.

Ingredients:

- 12 lasagna noodles
- 2 boneless, skinless chicken breasts (about 1 pound/450g), cooked and shredded
- 2 cups (500ml) Alfredo sauce (homemade or store-bought)
- 2 cups (200g) shredded mozzarella cheese
- 1 cup (100g) grated Parmesan cheese
- 2 tablespoons chopped fresh parsley (optional, for garnish)

Instructions:

Preparing the Lasagna Noodles:

Cook the lasagna noodles in a large pot of boiling salted water until they are al dente. Follow the package instructions, but slightly undercook the noodles as they will continue to cook during baking.

Drain the noodles and lay them out on a clean kitchen towel to prevent sticking.

Cooking and Shredding the Chicken:

Season the chicken breasts with salt and freshly ground black pepper.

In a skillet over medium-high heat, add a drizzle of olive oil and cook the seasoned chicken for about 6-8 minutes per side, or until it reaches an internal temperature of 165°F (74°C).

Once cooked, shred the chicken into bite-sized pieces using two forks. Set aside.

Assembling the Chicken Alfredo Lasagna:

Preheat the oven to 375°F (190°C).

In a 9x13-inch baking dish, spread a thin layer of Alfredo sauce on the bottom to prevent the noodles from sticking.

Create the first layer by placing four lasagna noodles side by side in the dish.

Spread a generous layer of Alfredo sauce over the noodles, ensuring they are fully covered.

Sprinkle a portion of shredded chicken over the sauce.

Add a layer of mozzarella and Parmesan cheese on top.

Repeat the layering process two more times, using the remaining lasagna noodles, Alfredo sauce, shredded chicken, and cheeses.

Baking the Chicken Alfredo Lasagna:

Cover the baking dish with aluminum foil, tenting it slightly to prevent the cheese from sticking to the foil.

Bake the lasagna in the preheated oven for about 25-30 minutes, or until the cheese is melted and bubbly.

Final Touches:

Remove the foil and continue baking for an additional 10-15 minutes or until the cheese on top turns golden brown and slightly crispy.

Garnish and Serve:

Let the Chicken Alfredo Lasagna rest for a few minutes before serving.

Garnish with chopped fresh parsley for a burst of color and freshness.

Serve and Enjoy:

Slice the Chicken Alfredo Lasagna into portions and serve it hot, savoring the layers of tender lasagna noodles, creamy Alfredo sauce, and flavorful shredded chicken.

Section 2: Making a Chicken Alfredo Lasagna from Scratch

Creating a Chicken Alfredo Lasagna from scratch involves making the Alfredo sauce and cooking the chicken:

Homemade Alfredo Sauce: To make the Alfredo sauce from scratch, you'll need:

- 1/2 cup (1 stick/113g) unsalted butter
- 2 cups (480ml) heavy cream
- 2 cups (200g) grated Parmesan cheese
- 4 cloves garlic, minced
- Salt and freshly ground black pepper to taste

Instructions:

In a saucepan over medium heat, melt the butter and sauté the minced garlic until fragrant.

Pour in the heavy cream, stirring constantly, and let it simmer gently for a few minutes until it starts to thicken.

Gradually add the grated Parmesan cheese to the sauce, stirring continuously until it's fully melted and the sauce becomes creamy and smooth.

Season with salt and freshly ground black pepper to taste.

Shredded Chicken: You can cook the chicken for the lasagna using the same method described in the previous chapters, seasoning it with salt and pepper and cooking it until it reaches an internal temperature of 165°F (74°C). Once cooked, shred the chicken using two forks.

By layering lasagna noodles with the homemade Alfredo sauce and shredded chicken, you'll create a Chicken Alfredo Lasagna that's a crowd-pleasing and hearty meal. Enjoy the delightful combination of tender pasta, creamy sauce, and savory chicken in each comforting bite. This Chicken Alfredo Lasagna is sure to become a family favorite and a standout dish at any gathering or celebration.

Chapter 17: Spinach and Chicken Alfredo Calzone

Section 1: Filling Pizza Dough with Alfredo Goodness

In this chapter, we'll explore a mouthwatering variation of Chicken Alfredo Pasta—Spinach and Chicken Alfredo Calzone. By using pizza dough as a delectable vessel, we fill it with the creamy Alfredo goodness, tender chicken, and nutritious spinach, creating a delightful handheld meal. Get ready to enjoy the irresistible combination of flavors and textures in this scrumptious calzone.

Ingredients:

- 1 pound (450g) pizza dough (store-bought or homemade)
- 1 boneless, skinless chicken breast (about 1/2 pound/225g), cooked and shredded
- 1 cup fresh spinach leaves, roughly chopped
- 1 cup (240ml) Alfredo sauce (homemade or store-bought)
- 1 cup (100g) shredded mozzarella cheese
- 1/2 cup (50g) grated Parmesan cheese
- 1/2 teaspoon garlic powder
- Olive oil, for brushing
- Fresh basil leaves, chopped (optional, for garnish)

Instructions:

Preparing the Pizza Dough:

If using store-bought pizza dough, follow the instructions on the package for allowing it to rise and come to room temperature.

If making homemade pizza dough, prepare the dough according to your favorite recipe and let it rise until doubled in size.

Cooking and Shredding the Chicken:

Season the chicken breast with salt and freshly ground black pepper.

In a skillet over medium-high heat, add a drizzle of olive oil and cook the seasoned chicken for about 6-8 minutes per side, or until it reaches an internal temperature of 165°F (74°C).

Once cooked, shred the chicken into bite-sized pieces using two forks. Set aside.

Creating the Spinach and Chicken Alfredo Filling:

In a mixing bowl, combine the shredded chicken, chopped spinach, Alfredo sauce, shredded mozzarella cheese, grated Parmesan cheese, and garlic powder. Mix everything well until the filling is thoroughly combined.

Assembling the Calzone:

Preheat the oven to 425°F (220°C).

On a lightly floured surface, roll out the pizza dough into a circle or rectangle, depending on your preference.

Transfer the rolled-out dough to a baking sheet lined with parchment paper.

Spoon the Spinach and Chicken Alfredo filling onto one half of the pizza dough, leaving a small border around the edges.

Fold the other half of the dough over the filling to form a semicircle, and press the edges together to seal the calzone.

Baking the Calzone:

Brush the top of the calzone with olive oil to give it a golden and crispy finish.

Use a knife to make a few small slits on top of the calzone to allow steam to escape while baking.

Bake the calzone in the preheated oven for about 20-25 minutes, or until the crust turns golden brown.

Garnish and Serve:

Remove the calzone from the oven and let it cool for a few minutes.

Garnish with chopped fresh basil leaves for a burst of color and freshness.

Serve and Enjoy:

Slice the Spinach and Chicken Alfredo Calzone into portions and serve it warm, savoring the delightful combination of creamy Alfredo sauce, tender chicken, and nutritious spinach.

Section 2: Baking a Delicious Calzone with Spinach and Chicken

To achieve a delicious Spinach and Chicken Alfredo Calzone, follow these tips:

Pizza Dough: Use a good-quality store-bought pizza dough or make your own using a reliable pizza dough recipe. Let the dough rise until it's doubled in size, and then roll it out into the desired shape.

Spinach: Use fresh spinach leaves for the filling. Wash and roughly chop them before incorporating them into the Alfredo sauce and chicken mixture.

Alfredo Sauce: You can use store-bought Alfredo sauce, but making your own from scratch using the recipe mentioned in previous chapters will add an extra level of flavor to the calzone.

Sealing the Calzone: Make sure to seal the calzone edges well to prevent the filling from leaking out during baking. You can use a fork to crimp the edges or fold them over and press down with your fingers.

By filling pizza dough with the delightful combination of Alfredo goodness, tender chicken, and nutritious spinach, you'll create a Spinach and Chicken Alfredo Calzone that's a flavorful and satisfying handheld meal. Enjoy the savory and creamy goodness of this delightful calzone, which is perfect for a quick lunch, dinner, or anytime you crave a comforting and delicious treat.

Chapter 18: Instant Pot Chicken Alfredo

Section 1: Speeding Up the Cooking Process with an Instant Pot

In this chapter, we'll explore a quick and efficient variation of Chicken Alfredo Pasta—Instant Pot Chicken Alfredo. By using the Instant Pot, we can significantly reduce the cooking time while still achieving the same creamy and flavorful results. Get ready to enjoy a delicious meal in a fraction of the time it takes to make the classic recipe.

Ingredients:

- 1 pound (450g) fettuccine pasta
- 2 boneless, skinless chicken breasts (about 1 pound/450g), cut into bite-sized pieces
- 2 cups (480ml) chicken broth
- 1 cup (240ml) heavy cream
- 1/2 cup (1 stick/113g) unsalted butter
- 1 cup (100g) grated Parmesan cheese
- 4 cloves garlic, minced
- Salt and freshly ground black pepper to taste
- Fresh parsley, chopped (optional, for garnish)

Instructions:

Sautéing the Chicken:

Set the Instant Pot to "Sauté" mode and add a drizzle of olive oil.

Season the chicken pieces with salt and freshly ground black pepper.

Sauté the seasoned chicken in the Instant Pot for about 2-3 minutes per side until it's lightly browned. Remove the chicken from the Instant Pot and set it aside.

Creating the Instant Pot Alfredo Sauce:

In the same Instant Pot, melt the unsalted butter.

Add the minced garlic and sauté for about a minute until it becomes fragrant.

Incorporating the Chicken Broth and Pasta:

Pour the chicken broth into the Instant Pot, stirring to deglaze the bottom of the pot and scrape up any browned bits.

Add the fettuccine pasta, ensuring it's fully submerged in the liquid.

Pressure Cooking:

Close the Instant Pot lid and set the vent to the sealing position.

Select the "Manual" or "Pressure Cook" setting and adjust the time to 6 minutes for al dente pasta.

Quick Pressure Release and Finishing the Sauce:

Once the pressure cooking is complete, perform a quick pressure release to safely open the Instant Pot.

Set the Instant Pot to "Sauté" mode again, and stir in the heavy cream and grated Parmesan cheese, allowing the sauce to thicken slightly.

Fold in the sautéed chicken, mixing it well with the Alfredo sauce.

Season and Garnish:

Taste the Instant Pot Chicken Alfredo and season with salt and freshly ground black pepper as needed.

Serve and Enjoy:

Garnish the Instant Pot Chicken Alfredo with chopped fresh parsley for a burst of color and freshness.

Serve the creamy and flavorful Instant Pot Chicken Alfredo hot and enjoy the wonderful result of this speedy adaptation.

Section 2: Adapting the Classic Recipe to the Pressure Cooker

To adapt the classic Chicken Alfredo Pasta recipe to the Instant Pot, follow these guidelines:

Sauté Function: Utilize the "Sauté" function on the Instant Pot to brown the chicken and sauté the garlic, which enhances the flavors of the dish.

Liquid Ratio: The ratio of chicken broth to pasta is essential for achieving the right consistency. In this recipe, 2 cups of chicken broth are used for 1 pound of fettuccine pasta.

Pressure Cooking Time: Cooking time in the Instant Pot is significantly shorter than traditional stovetop cooking. For fettuccine pasta, a pressure cooking time of 6 minutes is suitable for achieving an al dente texture.

Quick Pressure Release: To prevent overcooking the pasta, perform a quick pressure release as soon as the cooking time is up.

By adapting the classic Chicken Alfredo Pasta recipe to the Instant Pot, you'll enjoy a convenient and speedy cooking process without compromising on the deliciousness and creaminess of the dish. Savor the delightful combination of tender pasta, creamy Alfredo sauce, and savory chicken in this Instant Pot Chicken Alfredo, perfect for satisfying your pasta cravings in no time.

Chapter 19: Gluten-Free Chicken Alfredo
Section 1: Catering to Dietary Restrictions

In this chapter, we'll explore a delicious variation of Chicken Alfredo Pasta—Gluten-Free Chicken Alfredo. By using gluten-free pasta and alternative thickeners, we cater to individuals with dietary restrictions, ensuring everyone can enjoy this creamy and flavorful dish. Get ready to savor the same rich flavors and comforting goodness without the gluten.

Ingredients:

- 12 ounces (340g) gluten-free fettuccine pasta
- 2 boneless, skinless chicken breasts (about 1 pound/450g), cut into bite-sized pieces
- 1 cup (240ml) chicken broth (ensure it's gluten-free)
- 1 cup (240ml) heavy cream
- 1/2 cup (1 stick/113g) unsalted butter
- 1 cup (100g) grated Parmesan cheese (check for gluten-free labeling)
- 2 tablespoons cornstarch (or arrowroot powder for a corn-free option)
- 4 cloves garlic, minced
- Salt and freshly ground black pepper to taste
- Fresh parsley, chopped (optional, for garnish)

Instructions:

Cooking the Gluten-Free Pasta:

In a large pot, bring water to a boil and add a generous amount of salt. Cook the gluten-free fettuccine pasta according to the package instructions until al dente.

Once cooked, drain the pasta and set it aside.

Sautéing the Chicken:

Season the chicken pieces with salt and freshly ground black pepper.

In a skillet over medium-high heat, add a drizzle of olive oil. Cook the seasoned chicken for about 6-8 minutes per side, or until it reaches an internal temperature of 165°F (74°C).

Once cooked, remove the chicken from the skillet and set it aside.

Creating the Gluten-Free Alfredo Sauce:

In the same skillet used to cook the chicken, melt the unsalted butter over medium heat.

Add the minced garlic and sauté for about a minute until it becomes fragrant.

Incorporating the Chicken Broth and Heavy Cream:

Stir in the chicken broth, scraping any browned bits from the bottom of the skillet for added flavor.

Stir in the heavy cream and let the mixture simmer for a few minutes to thicken slightly.

Thicken the Sauce with Cornstarch or Arrowroot Powder:

In a small bowl, mix the cornstarch (or arrowroot powder) with a tablespoon of water to create a slurry.

Pour the slurry into the sauce, stirring continuously until it thickens to the desired consistency.

Add the Grated Parmesan Cheese:

Gradually add the grated Parmesan cheese to the sauce, stirring continuously until the cheese is fully melted, and the sauce becomes creamy and smooth.

Toss in the Pasta and Chicken:

Add the cooked gluten-free fettuccine pasta to the Alfredo sauce, tossing gently to coat the pasta evenly.

Fold in the cooked chicken pieces, ensuring they are well distributed throughout the pasta and sauce.

Season and Garnish:

Taste the Gluten-Free Chicken Alfredo and season with salt and freshly ground black pepper as needed.

Garnish and Serve:

Garnish the Gluten-Free Chicken Alfredo with chopped fresh parsley for a burst of color and freshness.

Serve and Enjoy:

Serve the creamy and flavorful Gluten-Free Chicken Alfredo hot and enjoy the wonderful result of catering to dietary restrictions.

Section 2: Using Gluten-Free Pasta and Alternative Thickeners

To create a gluten-free version of Chicken Alfredo Pasta, follow these guidelines:

Gluten-Free Pasta: Use a high-quality gluten-free fettuccine pasta made from rice, corn, quinoa, or other gluten-free grains. Cook it according to the package instructions until it's al dente.

Gluten-Free Chicken Broth: Make sure to use gluten-free chicken broth or homemade chicken broth made without gluten-containing ingredients.

Alternative Thickener: Instead of using all-purpose flour to thicken the sauce, use cornstarch or arrowroot powder. Mix the chosen thickener with water to create a slurry before adding it to the sauce.

By using gluten-free pasta and alternative thickeners, you'll create a delicious Gluten-Free Chicken Alfredo that's suitable for individuals with gluten sensitivities or celiac disease. Everyone can now enjoy the same creamy and flavorful dish without compromising on taste and satisfaction. Savor the delightful combination of tender pasta, creamy Alfredo sauce, and savory chicken in this gluten-free version, perfect for accommodating dietary restrictions while indulging in a comforting and delightful meal.

Chapter 20: Dessert Alfredo: Sweet Chocolate Fettuccine

Section 1: Ending on a Surprising Note with a Sweet Dish

In this final chapter, we'll take a delightful twist on the classic Chicken Alfredo Pasta and create a surprising dessert version—Sweet Chocolate Fettuccine. By transforming the savory Alfredo sauce into a sweet chocolate sauce and using fettuccine-like ribbons made of chocolate, we end our cookbook on a sweet and delightful note. Get ready to indulge in this unique and decadent dessert!

Ingredients:

For the Sweet Chocolate Fettuccine:

- 8 ounces (225g) dark chocolate, finely chopped
- 1/2 cup (120ml) heavy cream
- 1 tablespoon unsalted butter
- 1 teaspoon vanilla extract
- 8 ounces (225g) dried lasagna noodles (without salt)

For the Chocolate Whipped Cream:

- 1 cup (240ml) heavy cream
- 2 tablespoons powdered sugar
- 1/4 cup (30g) cocoa powder
- Chocolate shavings or grated chocolate, for garnish

Instructions:

Making the Sweet Chocolate Fettuccine:

Cook the dried lasagna noodles in a large pot of boiling water according to the package instructions. Cook them until they are al dente. (Note: Do not add salt to the water for this dessert version.)

Once cooked, drain the lasagna noodles and set them aside.

Creating the Sweet Chocolate Sauce:

In a saucepan over low heat, combine the heavy cream and unsalted butter. Heat the mixture until the butter is melted and the cream is warm.

Add the finely chopped dark chocolate to the warm cream and butter mixture.

Stir continuously until the chocolate is fully melted and the sauce becomes smooth and velvety.

Remove the saucepan from the heat and stir in the vanilla extract.

Coating the "Fettuccine" with Sweet Chocolate Sauce:

Using a pair of kitchen scissors, cut the cooked lasagna noodles into thin, ribbon-like strips, resembling fettuccine.

Transfer the "fettuccine" to a large bowl and pour the warm sweet chocolate sauce over the noodles.

Toss gently to coat the "fettuccine" evenly with the luscious chocolate sauce.

Making the Chocolate Whipped Cream:

In a separate mixing bowl, combine the heavy cream, powdered sugar, and cocoa powder.

Using an electric mixer, whip the cream until soft peaks form.

Serving the Sweet Chocolate Fettuccine:

Divide the coated "fettuccine" into individual serving bowls or plates.

Top each serving with a generous dollop of chocolate whipped cream.

Garnish with chocolate shavings or grated chocolate for an extra touch of elegance.

Serve and Enjoy:

Serve the Sweet Chocolate Fettuccine immediately, delighting in the surprising sweetness and decadence of this unique dessert.

Savor each bite of the creamy chocolate-coated "fettuccine" and the fluffy chocolate whipped cream.

Section 2: Preparing a Delightful Dessert Version of Alfredo Pasta

To create this delightful dessert version of Alfredo pasta, follow these guidelines:

Chocolate Selection: Use high-quality dark chocolate with at least 70% cocoa content to achieve a rich and indulgent chocolate flavor.

Ribbon-Like "Fettuccine": Cut the cooked lasagna noodles into thin, ribbon-like strips to resemble fettuccine. You can also use a vegetable peeler to create chocolate ribbons if desired

Chocolate Whipped Cream: Enhance the dessert with a chocolate whipped cream topping. Be sure to whip the cream until soft peaks form for a light and airy texture.

By transforming the classic Alfredo sauce into a sweet chocolate sauce and using chocolate ribbons in place of traditional pasta, you'll create a delightful and surprising dessert version—Sweet Chocolate Fettuccine. Enjoy the sweet decadence of this unique dessert, perfect for ending your meal on a delightful and unforgettable note. Indulge in the unexpected pleasure of creamy chocolate "fettuccine" coated in velvety sauce and topped with fluffy chocolate whipped cream, making this dessert a true treat for chocolate lovers and dessert enthusiasts alike.

In this cookbook, we embarked on a delicious culinary journey, exploring various creative and mouthwatering variations of the classic Chicken Alfredo Pasta. From traditional and authentic recipes to exciting twists, we covered a wide range of flavors and cooking techniques to satisfy different tastes and preferences.

We delved into the history and origin of Chicken Alfredo Pasta, understanding its roots in Italian cuisine and its popularity around the world. We explored the essential ingredients and cooking techniques that contribute to the creamy and flavorful Alfredo sauce, ensuring that you have a solid foundation to create the perfect dish.

Throughout the cookbook, we introduced exciting chapters that showcased delightful variations of Chicken Alfredo Pasta. We explored the richness of Garlic Butter Chicken Pasta, the fusion of Italian and American cuisines in Grilled Chicken Alfredo Pizza, and the spicy kick of Cajun Chicken Alfredo. We catered to vegetarian tastes with Mushroom and Chicken Alfredo, and brightened flavors with Lemon Pepper Chicken Alfredo. We simplified the cooking process with One-Pot Chicken Alfredo and added a nutritious twist with Broccoli and Chicken Alfredo. We even ventured into unique combinations like Pesto Chicken Alfredo, Spinach and Artichoke Chicken Alfredo, and Chicken Alfredo Stuffed Shells. To provide comfort and familiarity, we combined favorite flavors in Bacon and Ranch Chicken Alfredo and intensified the taste with Sun-Dried Tomato Chicken Alfredo.

To accommodate dietary restrictions, we crafted Gluten-Free Chicken Alfredo, ensuring that individuals with gluten sensitivities or celiac disease can also enjoy this delightful dish. We concluded on a surprising note with a sweet twist—Dessert Alfredo: Sweet Chocolate Fettuccine—transforming the classic savory dish into a decadent and delightful dessert.

As a writer, it has been a pleasure to guide you through this culinary adventure. I hope this cookbook inspires you to experiment with different flavors and techniques, creating your own variations and adaptations of Chicken Alfredo Pasta. Whether you are an experienced cook or a culinary enthusiast, there's always room for creativity and innovation in the kitchen.

Now, it's time to bring these delectable recipes to life in your kitchen. Embrace the joy of cooking, share these delightful dishes with your loved ones, and savor the wonderful experiences that food brings. From classic comfort to bold experimentation, Chicken Alfredo Pasta is a versatile canvas for culinary exploration. Enjoy the journey of taste and discovery, and remember, there are no limits when it comes to creating delicious and memorable meals. Happy cooking!